FENG SHUI

FOR THE HOME

EVELYN LIP

平安国际出版社

HEIAN INTERNATIONAL, INC.

by Evelyn Lip

© Illustrations: Evelyn Lip
© 1986 Times Editions Pte Ltd, Singapore

First American Edition 1990
Seventh American Edition 1998

HEIAN INTERNATIONAL, INC.
Publishers
1815 W. 205th Street, Suite 301
Torrance, CA 90501

ISBN 0-89346-327-2

Printed in Singapore

Contents

Preface **v**

Acknowledgements **vii**

1 Introduction to *Feng Shui* **1**

2 The Belief in *Feng Shui* **6**

3 Geomancy, Siting and Buildings **12**

4 The Methods of Assessing *Feng Shui* **26**

5 *Qi* Locations Until 2043 **31**

6 Geomancy and Interior Elements **43**

7 *Feng Shui* Room by Room **50**

8 *Feng Shui*, Interior Decor and Symbolism **60**

9 *Feng Shui* for the Office and Shophouse **71**

10 Garden Geomancy **78**

Bibliography **82**

To
Kenny and Jacqueline Lip

Preface

The Chinese have had a tremendously long and rich cultural history. Thousands of years ago the Chinese had already discovered how to cure illnesses through the prescription of herbs, how to eliminate pain through acupuncture and how to detect and utilise the energy of the earth to benefit mankind.

The energy of the natural forces of the earth can be detected through scientific and intuitive means, through the tangible and the intangible. About 1,600 years ago the Chinese had already determined that there were invisible forces beneath the earth. (These were later confirmed to be the magnetic forces of the earth.) The Chinese also believed that the forces were positive (*yang*) and negative (*yin*) and invented a magnetic compass called a *luopan* to measure them.

To the Chinese, there are energy lines or *qi* locations in the human body as well as in the earth. They believe there must be perfect balance of the positive and negative aspects of this energy in the human body, for perfect health, and in the earth, for the production of vibrant *qi*, or cosmic breath.

Qi in the body produces vitality, energy and balance of mind and body. *Qi* in the earth produces growth, regenerating spirit and harmony of natural forces. It is *qi* that enables people to perform feats of martial art and it is *qi* that promotes growth on the earth. *Feng shui* is the art of detecting this *qi* in a room, building or on any given site.

Although some of us do not ponder the totality of the universe, the solar system or the forces of the earth, we do concern ourselves with the tangible forces that affect our built environments. Our environment not only affects our physical well-being, it influences our sense of comfort and peace of mind. For instance, an extremely congested space makes the dweller uncomfortable and confused. And an awkward form or structure creates a sense of imbalance.

The colour, lighting and finishing of an interior also influence mood and well-being. When a room is painted in a warm colour, the user literally feels warmer. When lighting is subtly and appropriately designed, the user feels at ease and does not suffer from glare. When the interior finishes of a building are well applied, the users can feel the texture and pattern created.

Interior designers use texture, pattern, colour and light to give space its form and character, while geomancers attempt to balance the elements to give space *qi* and vitality. And geomancers focus on the detection of *qi* for placement of interior elements and furniture.

This book aims to explain the interaction between the tangible and intangible aspects of an interior, or how the design and placement of interior elements and the detection and use of *qi* work together to attain visual and cosmic harmony. Moreover, it will help the reader find and capture the favourable cosmic breath in a house, apartment, office, shophouse and garden, and use it to achieve good health and vitality.

Acknowledgements

I am indebted to my readers all over the world who have shown tremendous interest in *feng shui*. Much of the inspiration for this book comes from these readers and other enthusiastic people from numerous organisations and universities who have invited me to talk on topics related to my first book, *Chinese Geomancy*, and my other publications. Their interest and enthusiasm have given me tremendous moral support and encouragement to write another book on the subject of *feng shui*. I wish to thank Durham, Jessica, Carolyn and many other such encouraging readers.

I acknowledge all those who have given me permission to publish case studies and resource materials. Special thanks go to Mr. K.H. Lim and Mr. S.K. Saw who have discussed the theory of *feng shui* with me on two occasions. I also wish to thank the managers of Dragon City for granting me permission to publish a photograph of the interior of their restaurant.

I wish to acknowledge the confidence and inspiration Miss Shirley Hew has given me in making this book a useful reference for those who wish to know about *feng shui* and the interior layout of their homes. I am grateful to Jane Kohen Winter for her inspiring comments and appropriate advice given during the course of writing this manuscript.

Thanks also go to my son Kenny Lip who has spent many hours typing the manuscript and taking photographs. Last, but not least, I wish to thank the members of my immediate family, Francis, Kenny and Jacqueline, for their inspiring comments, and my mother, brother and relatives Peng, Seng, Lynn, and Fatt and friends (especially S.C. Lim, C.P. Chavy, Y.T. Lu,) for their moral support and encouragement during the course of writing this book.

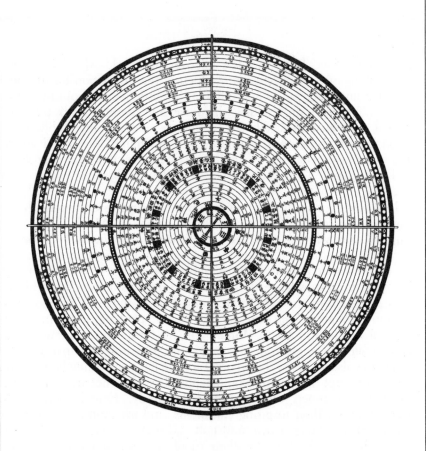

A *compass* or luopan *is used for geomantic assessment.*

1 Introduction to *Feng Shui*

Feng shui （风水） is the art of placement of things, ranging from the orientation of buildings to the furnishing of interiors, to influence the *qi* （气） or cosmic breath of a site. *Feng shui* helps man utilise the earth's natural forces and balance *yin* and *yang* to achieve good *qi*, which renders health and vitality. Very often, good *feng shui* is achieved through the combination of common sense and good taste in the conception of space, placement of furniture and best use of structure. Excellent living conditions contribute to good health, which often leads to success and prosperity.

Feng shui is also known as Chinese geomancy. Many ancient cities were geomantically planned within the *qi* or dragon energy of the mountain ranges. For example, Louyang, once the cultural heart and capital of ancient China, was believed to be within the beneficial *qi* of the *Kunlun Shan* （崑崙山）, a mountain range, and was sustained by the balance of the *yin* （阴） and *yang* （阳） forces.

The capital of the Ming period, Yan Shan （燕山）, was situated in the midstream of the *qi* of *Kunlun*. *Tai Shan* （泰山）, the "azure dragon" （青龙）, was on the left; *Hua Shan* （华山）, the "white tiger" （白虎）, was on the right; and *Song Shan* （嵩山） formed the protective mountain ranges at the back.

In fact, the imperial cities and palaces of China were planned in accordance with the precepts of *feng shui*. For example, the Forbidden City built by the Ming emperor and rebuilt by the Qing ruler was very much based on geomantic principles. The palace was symmetrical with north/south orientation, and the main gate facing south. A south orientation was preferable because the wind from Mongolia carried a great deal of yellow dust and was terribly cold. People avoided placing windows on the north, and such practice became common. Even now, many Beijing houses do not have windows or other openings on the north.

The entire Forbidden City was enclosed by a moat so that water flowed past the main gate and entrance. This was done because, to the Chinese, water symbolises wealth. (Water flowing past the main door was like receiving wealth.) In addition, the *Tai He Dian* （太和殿）, *Zhong He Dian* （中和殿）, *Bao He Dian* （宝和殿） and the rest of the palaces were given "backing" by a hill which was manmade for good *feng shui*. Backing in this context means protection, especially against wind and cold.

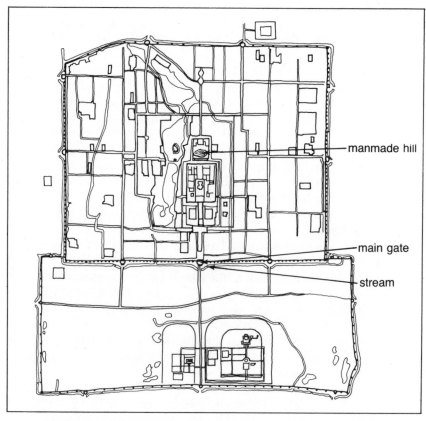

The Forbidden City had good feng shui *because it was protected by a manmade hill and a stream ran past the main gate.*

The *Tai He Men* （太和门）, or door to the first palace, was purposely placed in front of the Golden Water Stream. The gate had nine colonnades (nine symbolises longevity), and the entire palace complex was decorated in auspicious colours and motifs. Dragons (*yang* symbols), pearls (*yin* symbols), quadrupeds and flowers were made and placed on the roofs and walls as symbols of good fortune and success.

The entire setting and planning of the Summer Palace was also based on *feng shui* precepts. The palace was built overlooking the *Kun Ming Lake* （昆明湖） on a slope with the hills in the north as backing.

Hills or mountains should back a site to form a protective shield.

3

Although *feng shui* was "invented" in China almost 3,000 years ago, it spread to Japan and other southeastern regions more than a thousand years ago. In fact, Nara and Kyoto became capitals because of the good *feng shui* of the sites. Many Chinese and other Asians applied and still apply the art of *feng shui* to the interior and exteriors of buildings to achieve harmony and balance.

Geomancers advocate that everything in nature has life and animistic characteristics similar to the shape or type of animal resembled. For example, a hill that looks like a tortoise is a good site because people who live on it enjoy longevity just like the tortoise. And a mountain shaped like a dragon renders strength and cosmic breath to the inhabitants of that region.

To the Chinese, everything contains living organisms and everything has a particular environment and condition in which it can best exist. Man is no different from other organisms; he has an optimal situation in which he can succeed to his fullest capacity. Chinese geomancy is the art of finding and providing such a situation, or living in tune with the natural setting and the energy of the earth, rather than fighting the laws of nature.

Feng Shui *in Perspective*

As far back as the twelfth century B.C., the Chinese had already established the order of the Five Elements 五行 (gold 金, wood 木, water 水, fire 火, and earth 土) which provided their concepts of the world. Everything in the world, they thought, was associated with one of these Five Elements.

By the second century A.D., the Chinese had already noted the principal constellations and the planets. They had also established the revolution of the planets around the sun. A century later, martial artists and Taoists developed the art of control of the body energy *qi* for the performance of supernatural feats. Many Taoists and Confucianists were also well-versed in geography, and were known as *Di Li Jia* (地理家) or geographers. They were the first to start the form and compass schools of geomancy, and created the art of living in harmony with the earth and the heavens.

By the eighth century, the first Chinese magnetic compass for seafaring was invented. During the same period, Chinese medicine based on the principles of *yin* and *yang* foods was used to treat illnesses. The magnetic compass was incorporated into a diviner's board and became the *luopan* (罗盘), which is the geomancer's compass. By the ninth century, a compass was made for the siting of tombs, and in the twelfth century, another plate, the Inner Heaven Plate, was added to the *luopan* to divinate on the houses of the living.

As you can see, China has had a rich cultural history. The discovery of the art of *feng shui*, though ancient, can still be used to guide us in building and furniture placement, even though the geography and 'climate of the part of the world we live in is different from China. Do we still have to orient our windows and doors to avoid the north wind blowing from Mongolia? Must we live near water to be successful? Moreover, must we hire a geomancer to tell us where and how to live?

Although some homeowners can afford to pay geomancers for their services, many cannot or are unable to find suitable *feng shui* experts to improve their dwellings. Many flat dwellers think they cannot benefit from *feng shui* because they are unable to shift their front doors or re-orient their dwellings. Some even choose to move to new flats that have better *feng shui*.

My aim in writing this book is to alleviate the fears shared by many flat and home dwellers, and to encourage them to place the interior elements in their homes according to geomantic principles, despite the fact that structural re-orientation is impossible. Even though flat dwellers cannot control the external environment, they can control the internal usage of space. By locating the *qi* in their flats, and placing important activities in the *qi* areas, anyone can benefit from the revitalising breath of the earth.

2 The Belief in *Feng Shui*

The Chinese have based their practice of medicine, their art of cooking, theory of martial art, and practice of *feng shui* on the *yin* and *yang* philosophy. Even the words *feng* （风）, which means wind, and *shui* （水）, which means water, are derived from the trigrams of *yang* and *yin*.

For thousands of years the Chinese have based their divination of the future on the working of the *Yi-Jing* （易经）, the planetary movement, and the magnetism of the earth in relation to the horoscopes and the natural forces of *yin* and *yang*. The practice of Chinese medicine and acupuncture is based on the balance of *yin* and *yang* energy within the human body. Should an internal organ be suffering from the imbalance of *yin* and *yang*, the acupuncturist inserts a needle at the appropriate point in the body to revitalise the energy points and achieve balance.

Chinese food is also classified under *yin* and *yang*. A person should eat a balanced amount of *yin* (cooling) food and *yang* (heaty) food. Should there be too much *yin*, a *yang* herb should be eaten to give balance (and vice versa), or the person might fall sick.

Many forms of martial art are also founded on the *yin-yang* theory. *Tai ji* （太极） and *wu ji* （无级）, for example, are based on the action of balancing on either the *yin* (left) or the *yang* (right) foot. This belief in the idea of balance has survived for thousands of years.

The Influence of Feng Shui

Feng shui has also survived the test of time. It has exerted its influence on numerous people and puzzled countless architects, interior designers and developers. In Singapore, many hotels and high-rise developments have been designed according to the advice of local geomancers, as well as those from Hong Kong and Taiwan. In general, geomancers do extremely well in business. Each consultation costs from S$500 to S$5,000, and some geomancers are said to earn S$50,000 a month. In Hong Kong, some geomancers charge by the square metre of the built-in area they assess.

Managers of the well-known Hyatt Hotel in Singapore are reputed to have employed the services of a famous geomancer for the alteration of the doors, fountains and the information counter. After the alterations, business improved.

Some practising architects have encountered clients who insist on altering building plans for better *feng shui*. Sometimes, construction is held at a standstill so the main door and ridge beam can be installed at just the right moment (according to the geomancer's calculations and the year of birth of the owner).

Business managers often consult geomancers for the placement of their work-tables and sofas. And geomancers are often employed to measure work-tables to make sure they are of a lucky dimension. Should the measurement be unlucky, the geomancer will alter the size of the piece. Housewives also consult geomancers for the placement of their beds — for good luck and to ensure conception of desirable children.

I encountered geomancers on numerous occasions during my practice of architecture in the 1960's. When I first returned from London in 1966 I was given a large house to design. The client's family, including the mother-in-law, approved my sketches with delight and appreciation on my first presentation. But one week later, the client returned with an elderly man who was introduced as a *feng shui* master. Before the meeting was over, the plan of the house was torn to bits.

The staircase that originally faced the entrance hall was hidden and enclosed by walls. The front door was tilted to capture luck, and the storeroom was moved to a new position to be in harmony with the fire element so the house wouldn't encounter ill luck.

This incident was only the beginning of a series of cultural shocks for a young architect. During my next few years of practice, I experienced numerous disagreements with geomancers. Before I understood the precepts of *feng shui* I designed a house facing a hill with the main staircase fronting the main door and the main gate situated on a T-junction. For years the tenants of the house suffered calamities. By 1977 I was determined to find out all I could about *feng shui* and its influence on buildings and interiors. I searched for knowledge from Qing dynasty and ancient classical writings on geomancy.

I even carried out experiments to study the way *qi* flows through the front door of a house. Using a small tank filled with water and an electric motor, I used waves to simulate the flow of *qi* in different situations. From my experiments I concluded that:

- *qi* best enters the house through the main door when there is no obstruction in front of the opening of a house;
- obstructions such as lamp posts placed in front of the main door can disrupt the entry of *qi* into the house and create imbalance;
- when there is an obstruction on one side of the house, the ill effects can be lessened by placing another on the other side to achieve balance;
- and the orientation of the main door affects the entry of *qi* into the house.

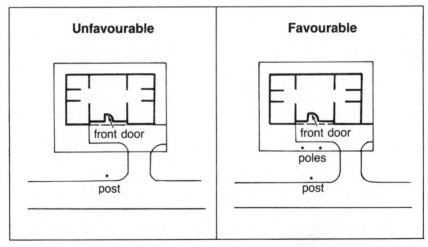

A single lamp post or pole outside the front door of a dwelling can create an imbalance of qi. *Harmony can be achieved by placing two posts as shown to counterbalance the original post.*

My conclusions can be illustrated by the true story of a rich Hong Kong businessman who built a mansion facing the sea for his family. In all respects the mansion was luxurious, but somehow the family members suffered from bad luck. Within a few years the children died from illnesses. The wife too was seriously ill and the businessman lost money in his business ventures.

He finally engaged a geomancer to assess the *feng shui* of the house, but he could find nothing wrong. A few months later the businessman's wife passed away. Again he sought the advice of geomancers but none could help him. Finally, a geomancer recommended by a friend offered his services. The businessman insisted that he stay in the house for a week. Each day, the geomancer studied the house, but he too could find nothing wrong.

On the last day of his stay, the geomancer got up very early and carefully examined the surrounding environment of the house. The tide was low and to the geomancer's surprise he saw a rock in the sea facing the house. The rock was shaped like a huge frog with its mouth wide open. The geomancer reported his finding to the businessman who insisted that the rock be destroyed. Unfortunately, no matter how hard they tried, the workmen could not blow up the rock. Eventually, the businessman also became ill, but managed to recover after moving from the house, which, it appears, was left vacant for years.

Other reports on the influence of *feng shui* are widespread. For instance, in 1982 the *New Straits Times* in Kuala Lumpur reported that the main gate of a certain television station was barred because employees believed the pathway to have bad *feng shui* and preferred to use the side entrance. And when a leading bank in the city moved its headquarters, a geomancer was hired to advise on the position and placement of the stone lions.

In Hong Kong, a London-trained senior architect in the Public Works Department claimed that six new towns in the New Territories — housing 1.8 million people — were designed according to *feng shui* principles. In 1981, a news report mentioned that Hong Kong's colonial masters had spent more than HK$1.5 million for a geomancer to relocate

ancestral graves. And when a 1985 edition of *The Star* reported that a mentally ill man in Kowloon killed four children and injured 30 at a kindergarten, a *feng shui* master said it was due to an industrial chimney directly opposite the kindergarten. The chimney, he said, looked like the incense sticks burned at funerals.

The November issue of an international magazine reported that the architect of the Regent Hotel in Hong Kong decided to consult a geomancer regarding the plans of the hotel before it opened in 1982. As a result, a glass wall 12 metres high was built to give the nine dragons access to the harbour. It is said that even the management of the Hongkong and Shanghai Banking Corporation consulted a geomancer before plans were drawn for a new bank.

Again in Kuala Lumpur, *feng shui* was considered when many of the shopping complexes were built. The Sungai Wang Plaza for instance, was built on a hill and its entrance was placed to avoid facing the road.

According to one geomancer, the Hong Kong businessman who had a frog-shaped obstruction blocking the flow of qi through his main door might have been helped if stone flies sculpted from rock had been placed in the mouth of the frog.

The MAS headquarters, Promet Tower and the MUI Plaza were placed in such a way that there was harmony and neutrality among the buildings in that area.

Despite the expertise and reliability of many *feng shui* experts, it is not advisable to blindly rely on *feng shui* to remedy all bad situations. For example, I was told that a man went through years of frustration because his geomancer advised him that he would enjoy rapid promotion if he drove up steps every evening on his return from work. (In Chinese, going "up the steps" is analogous for getting promoted.) It turns out that the man did not get the promotion he wished, but had to spend a great deal of money in the frequent replacement of his tyres.

In another strange case, a man slept with a mirror under a cushion because his geomancer told him it would make him more intelligent. All the man learned, it seems, was that sleeping on a mirror gave him a stiff neck!

It should also be mentioned that different geomancers have different approaches to geomancy, and that not all approaches can improve *feng shui*. In fact, the most important factor lies in the moral character of the person seeking advice. If he is evil or immoral, his good *feng shui* will not last.

3 Geomancy, Siting and Buildings

Before the homeowner or flat dweller can begin to apply *feng shui* principles to his or her interior environment, it is necessary to become familiar with the geomantic theory of the outside environment. Although it is still possible to benefit from the revitalising breath of *qi* without altering the external environment, it is important to understand the totality of geomantic theory, and to see the consistency between the principles of *feng shui* in and outside the home.

In general, there are several rules of thumb that the geomancer uses to intuitively assess the *feng shui* of a site. Some of the rules are as follows:

- a building constructed on elevated ground, facing a slow moving river or serene lake is well-located, and should benefit from cosmic *qi*.

- a house facing a vacant lot on the south is good geomantically because in China, during the summer, the south winds are refreshing and bring good ventilation or cosmic breath.

- on the contrary, a house facing northeast is not good because the northerly winds bring yellow dust from Mongolia.

- the front portion of a building or a town should be lower than the back. The front should face a valley, sea or lower ground, and the back should face a hill, mountain or higher ground so that the structure or town has ample protection and captures cosmic breath. A plot of land with a fairly good view in front and slightly elevated ground at the back is considered fairly good.

- the site must have fairly clean top-soil and drainage must be efficient.

- trees should be planted to make the site pleasant, to give it a sense of privacy, and to act as a buffer against noise from the main road. Too many trees can block the much-needed sunlight from the interior of the house, and disrupt the flow of *qi*.

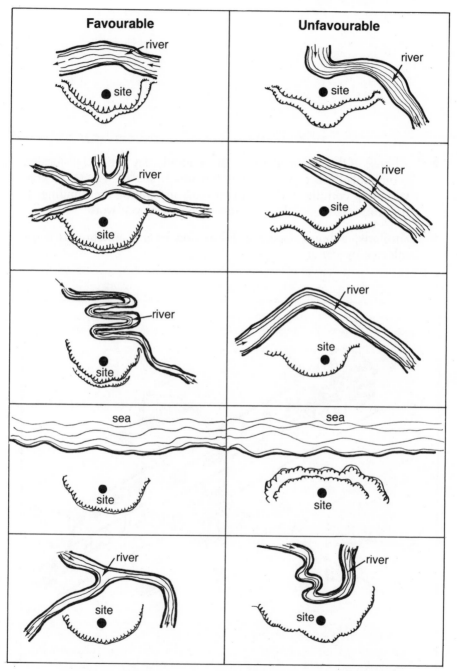

| Favourable | Unfavourable |

The direction and flow of water courses have both favourable and unfavourable effects on feng shui.

- a house at the end of a cul-de-sac or blind alley is not well-located geomantically because there is too much *sha qi* （杀气）or very vibrant *qi* coming from the main road and hitting the building. If the front door faces the road the situation is even worse.

- similarly, a house facing a T-junction or a Y-junction is badly affected by *sha qi*.

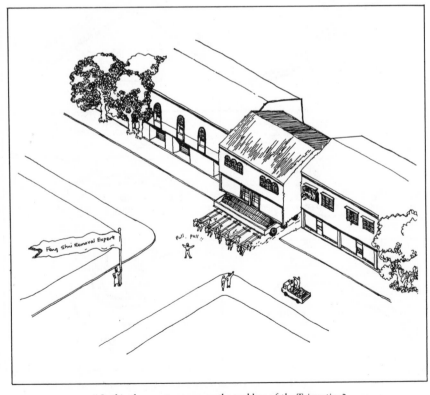

Is this the way to overcome the problem of the T-junction?

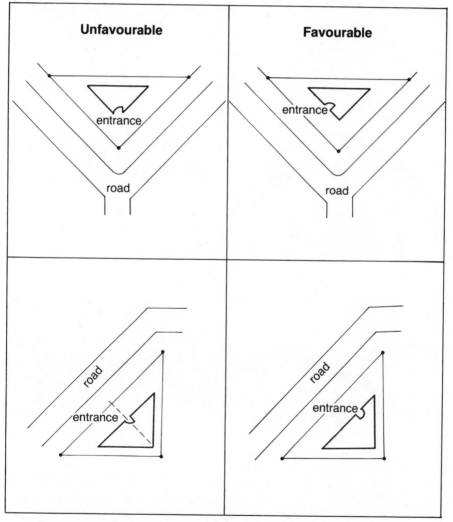

It is not wise to place the entrance of a building facing a Y-junction or directly in the middle of the top of the Y shape.

The shapes of surrounding hills affect the feng shui of a site.

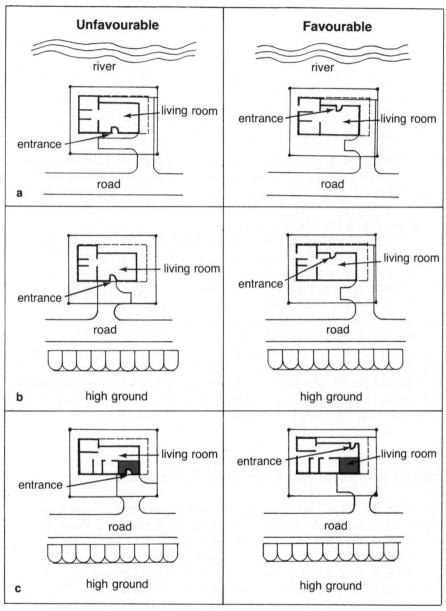

(a) *When a building is situated so its rear faces a body of water, the entrance should be placed at the rear of the site.*
(b) *If the site faces higher ground, the entrance is also better placed at the rear of the site.*
(c) *If the qi area (in red) is located at the front of a site which faces a hill, a compromise should be made by using the qi area for the master bedroom or living room.*

In Southeast Asia there are numerous examples of Chinese temples constructed under the influence of geomancy. In 1852 for instance, *Wak Hai Cheng Bio (Yue Hai Cheng Miao)*, a Chinese temple on Phillip Street in Singapore, was designed with reference to its surrounding high and low ground and nearby water courses.

The *Guan Yin Tang* temple at Telok Blangah Drive in Singapore is an excellent example of a Chinese temple with good *feng shui*. Built in 1886, the temple is situated on high ground overlooking the sea, and benefitting from the *yang* of the lower vacant ground in front. It is protected on the sides and at the back by hilly ground, and is in accordance with the Chinese saying *"zuo shan wang hai"* (坐山望海) , or "sitting on the hill overlooking the sea."

And *Ji Le Si* in Penang is built on a hill that looks like a flying stork, which is associated with longevity. The site is nearly perfect geomantically because the Dragon Hill is on the left, and the White Elephant Hill on the right. Similarly, *San Bao Dong* in Ipoh sits on a site that has an entrance like the head of a dragon and an airwell at the rear that resembles the tail of a dragon.

Feng Shui *and the Exterior of Buildings*

Buildings should be designed with both environmental and *feng shui* principles in mind. When a building is designed without proper protection, rain will penetrate the interior and dampness will spoil the internal finishes. If the roof is not designed at the appropriate angle, rain water will seep in. It is not surprising that the Chinese have always designed their buildings to withstand heavy rain and wind. Their roof overhangs are built very large to protect the walls of the buildings from rain, wind and the summer sun.

Buildings in the tropics should be oriented in such a way that they benefit from cross breezes, so the interiors are cool and comfortable. In China, buildings are oriented facing south to capture the sunshine and to avoid the cold north wind that carries the yellow dust from the

Mongolian border. In Singapore it is best to orient a building north/south because of the path of the sun. However, some may prefer to place their buildings according to their horoscopes.

The layout of the buildings should also be in harmony with the surrounding environment and in balance with the neighbouring blocks. For example, a row of shophouses should be designed so that one shop does not stand out in terms of height or width. If this happens, the one in disharmony will not have good *feng shui*.

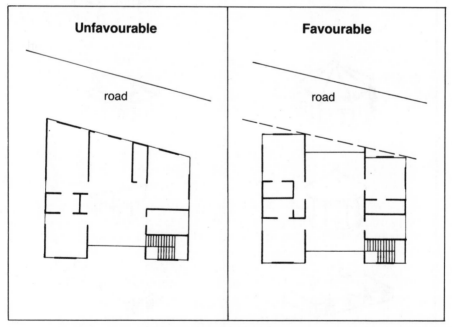

If a site is slanted, the building should not be designed with parallel walls to mimic it.

The geomancer considers the roof an important feng shui *element. Different shapes can have good and bad effects on* feng shui.

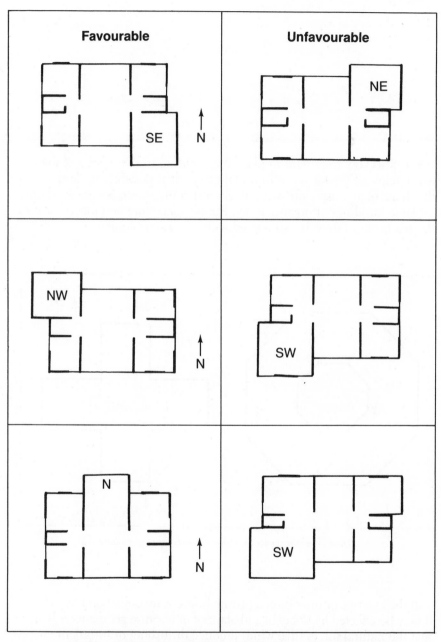

Building projections have favourable and unfavourable effects on feng shui. A projection on the northwest or southeast of a building, for example, brings wealth and luck to the tenants. A projection limited to one-third of the total length of a building on the north or east brings good luck to the tenants and a projection on the northeast or southwest is unlucky.

It is also very important to place the building in the *qi* area of the site (see Chapter Five for more information) and, if possible, to design it in the shape of an auspicious symbol. Some geometric shapes are good only for large buildings or organisations. Round shapes are best placed next to the sea because they are associated with the water element.

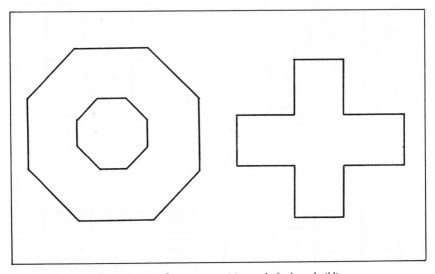

These geometric shapes are auspicious only for large buildings.

If the exterior or interior of a private house is modelled on these shapes it may be affected by *sha qi* or imbalanced *qi* because geomancers believe that the natural forces (like wind) produce disturbing or turbulent energy and pressure on the sides of the geometric shape. A small house may not be able to overcome the *sha qi* of the forces the way a multi-storey structure can.

The rules-of-thumb regarding the shapes of buildings or internal spaces are as follows:

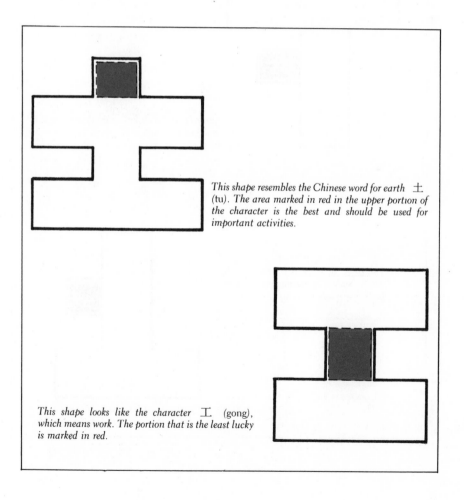

This shape resembles the Chinese word for earth 土 *(tu). The area marked in red in the upper portion of the character is the best and should be used for important activities.*

This shape looks like the character 工 *(gong), which means work. The portion that is the least lucky is marked in red.*

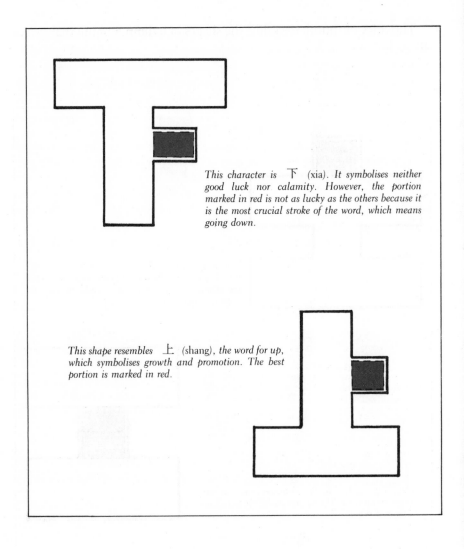

This character is 下 (xia). It symbolises neither good luck nor calamity. However, the portion marked in red is not as lucky as the others because it is the most crucial stroke of the word, which means going down.

This shape resembles 上 (shang), the word for up, which symbolises growth and promotion. The best portion is marked in red.

The *Tong Shu* or Chinese almanac should be consulted for an auspicious date to complete the building of a city or house. The date for the official opening of a business establishment has to be chosen by a geomancer so the horoscope of the managing director and the chosen time do not clash.

It is not wise to ignore architectural and environmental principles for the sake of *feng shui*. Very often, good *feng shui* is synonymous with good architecture, and vice versa. Sometimes, however, neither good architecture nor good *feng shui* can help a person's luck. The Chinese believe that our lives are predestined, and that we have certain lucky and unlucky spells. During our lucky spells, poor *feng shui* cannot affect us, but during our unlucky periods, very poor *feng shui* can make our situations even worse. When a person's luck is good, the Chinese say his *sha qi* is strong and able to overcome *sha qi* from poor *feng shui* and bad environmental influences. In fact, the ancient Chinese saying, "*Yi ming, er yun, san feng shui, si de, wu du shu*" (一命， 二运， 三风水， 四德， 五读书）, means "the most important factors influencing a person's life are fate first, luck second, *feng shui* third, virtue fourth, and education fifth."

4 The Methods of Assessing *Feng Shui*

There are basically two methods of assessing the *feng shui* of a site or an interior: the intuitive or form school method and the compass method. The former is based on the physical features or topographical characteristics of the land, while the latter is a more technical approach based on the *luopan*. Presently, geomancers tend to combine the two methods, although they consider the intuitive assessment of prime importance.

The intuitive or form school of geomancy stipulates that land should be undulating, with twists, turns and hills, because this indicates the dragon's *qi* or energy, and means the land is teeming with life. The Chinese regard a mountain or hill as a dragon because of the *qi* it holds. For example, Kowloon is considered good because it is built on a range of eight hills.

There are two theories on how Kowloon, which actually means nine dragons, got its name. One source says that people began calling the island *Jiu Long* because they counted a young emperor who used to live there as the ninth dragon. Another myth says that Kowloon was so named because of the suicide of the last Song ruler. It appears that after the Mongolian forces had invaded the Song Kingdom, the emperor was asked to locate a site with nine dragons to rebuild his kingdom. After some difficulty, he arrived at Kowloon, but to his disappointment he saw only eight hills (or eight dragons). In despair he jumped into the sea, not realising that he could have counted himself as the ninth dragon. So Kowloon, it is said, was named to commemorate his death.

According to the intuitive school of geomancy, besides undulating surfaces, good geomantic land must have fertile soil of many colours ranging from red to yellowish. It must also be protected by high hills at the back, and the hills must have smooth ridge profiles. Hills with pointed or sharp ridges are unlucky. The earth and sand of the site must be of good quality, and the site must be in a certain relationship to water courses or the sea. (See Chapter Three for more information.)

An excellent example of good geomantic land is the burial ground of Chinese Nationalist leader Sun Yat Sen's ancestors in Hong Kong: it is on a hill, embraced by high ground and facing the sea. (Constructing buildings on high ground is not exclusively a Chinese practice. It is done by Greeks, Romans, and other Europeans. Even villagers in Indonesia construct their chieftain's house on the highest ground so it is nearer to the lowest tier of heaven.)

The Luopan

For the compass method of geomantic assessment, a *luopan* is used to determine the flow of *qi* and the orientation of buildings, rooms and furniture. There are many types of *luopan*. Some are very simple and consist of only a few rings with a magnetised needle in the centre. Some are more complicated and contain 36 rings. The luopan is circular (symbolising heaven), made of wood (which may be lacquered or finished in metal), and set into a square board (symbolising earth).

The various rings are designed according to directional and cosmological systems. The inner ring is used to detect and evaluate water courses. The third ring gives the direction and cardinal points, and the fourth is based on the *Le Shu* (洛书) , which describes the nine rooms once used by the emperor during the different seasons of the year. Rings beyond this point describe the names of spirits. Ring seven, for instance, describes the 24 *shan* (山) while ring eight is used as a simple method of divination based on the changes in the positions of stars in every 20-year cycle of time. (This method, called *San Yuan Di Li* 三元地理 , is often used in addition to the intuitive and compass methods to detect the *qi* of a site or room.)

In using the *luopan* to determine the *feng shui* of a site or interior, the first step is to establish the north point. In a house which has been occupied for some time, it is rather difficult to establish the magnetic north because the interior may be cluttered with all kinds of metallic articles which can affect the needle. In this situation, the geomancer often goes outside the house, preferably on surrounding empty land, to establish the north point. In places where houses are packed very closely together, the geomancer may determine the north point through mathematical calculations based on the angle of the sun.

When the geomancer is able to use his *luopan* indoors, he keeps at least one metre from reinforced concrete columns or beams to avoid deflection. He holds the compass level with the floor and faces the direction being assessed, turning the *luopan* wheel until the magnetic needle of the compass overlaps the red line beneath the needle. He only reads the compass when the needle is stable.

In addition to the *luopan*, the geomancer's ruler is used to measure the length, breadth and height of building interiors and furnishings. Good dimensions include:

- 0 to 5⅜ centimetres
- 16⅛ to 26⅞ cm
- 37⅝ to 48⅜ cm
- multiples of 43 cm (e.g. 4300 or 4343) or multiples of 43 cm added to any of the above measurements

Bad dimensions include:
- 5⅜ to 16⅛ cm
- 26⅞ to 37⅝ cm
- multiples of 43 cm added to the above measurements

The compass method of determining the geomantic quality of a site is also based on the working of the *Yi-Jing* and the Eight Trigrams, as well as the *luopan*. For interior design, the *luopan* is used in conjunction with the *San Yuan* mentioned earlier, and the *Le Shu*, which is based on the movement of the planetary system.

Orientation is also considered very important when assessing a site or building. Geomancers use the accompanying charts, which relate orientation to year of birth, to place the main door of a house and the beds of the occupants. As you can see, orientation for males is different from that for females.

	Qi orientations for males								
	SW	**E**	**SE**	**SW**	**NW**	**W**	**NE**	**S**	**N**
Year of birth	1917	1916	1915	1914	1913	1912	1911	1910	1909
	1926	1925	1924	1923	1922	1921	1920	1919	1918
	1935	1934	1933	1932	1931	1930	1929	1928	1927
	1944	1943	1942	1941	1940	1939	1938	1937	1936
	1953	1952	1951	1950	1949	1948	1947	1946	1945
	1962	1961	1960	1959	1958	1957	1956	1955	1954
	1971	1970	1969	1968	1967	1966	1965	1964	1963
	1980	1979	1978	1977	1976	1975	1974	1973	1972
	1989	1988	1987	1986	1985	1984	1983	1982	1981
	1998	1997	1996	1995	1994	1993	1992	1991	1990
	2007	2006	2005	2004	2003	2002	2001	2000	1999
	2016	2015	2014	2013	2012	2011	2010	2009	2008
	2025	2024	2023	2022	2021	2020	2019	2018	2017
	2034	2033	2032	2031	2030	2029	2028	2027	2026
	2043	2042	2041	2040	2039	2038	2037	2036	2035
	2052	2051	2050	2049	2048	2047	2046	2045	2044

	Qi orientations for females								
	SE	**E**	**SW**	**N**	**S**	**NE**	**W**	**NW**	**NW**
Year of birth	1917	1916	1915	1914	1913	1912	1911	1910	1909
	1926	1925	1924	1923	1922	1921	1920	1919	1918
	1935	1934	1933	1932	1931	1930	1929	1928	1927
	1944	1943	1942	1941	1940	1939	1938	1937	1936
	1953	1952	1951	1950	1949	1948	1947	1946	1945
	1962	1961	1960	1959	1958	1957	1956	1955	1954
	1971	1970	1969	1968	1967	1966	1965	1964	1963
	1980	1979	1978	1977	1976	1975	1974	1973	1972
	1989	1988	1987	1986	1985	1984	1983	1982	1981
	1998	1997	1996	1995	1994	1993	1992	1991	1990
	2007	2006	2005	2004	2003	2002	2001	2000	1999
	2016	2015	2014	2013	2012	2011	2010	2009	2008
	2025	2024	2023	2022	2021	2020	2019	2018	2017
	2034	2033	2032	2031	2030	2029	2028	2027	2026
	2043	2042	2041	2040	2039	2038	2037	2036	2035
	2052	2051	2050	2049	2048	2047	2046	2045	2044

To use the chart, first find your date of birth and trace your finger to the top of the column to find your orientation. For example, if you are a man born in 1949, your orientation is northwest. Therefore, your front door should be placed northwest.

This also means that the important areas of the house (e.g. the bedrooms and living rooms) should be placed with reference to the recommended orientation, and the unimportant areas (the kitchen and toilets) should be located away from the recommended orientation. The geomancer considers the bedroom, living room, dining room and storage (or safe) as areas that can benefit from the *qi* of the earth. (Geomancers believe that *qi*, in fact, centres in the dining area.) The toilets and kitchen cannot benefit from *qi*, and if wrongly placed, may exert *si qi* （死气） or dead *qi*, and affect the *feng shui* of the entire house.

No matter what your orientation, toilets and kitchens should not be placed in the north because traditionally, the Chinese have reserved the north for the masters and the south for the servants. Since the northeast and southwest directions have been called the *gui men* (or doors of the devil), geomancers always place the toilets, kitchen and staircases away from those directions. Many houses in Beijing were designed this way.

Although many geomancers decide the orientation of the front door using the chart above, other geomancers use the time of birth rather than the year of birth as a reference.

Animal symbol related to time of birth	Hour of birth	Orientation
Dragon	7 am − 9 am	ESE
Snake	9 am − 11 am	SSE
Horse	11 am − 1 pm	S
Sheep	1 pm − 3 pm	SSW
Monkey	3 pm − 5 pm	WSW
Cock	5 pm − 7 pm	W
Dog	7 pm − 9 pm	WNW
Pig	9 pm − 11 pm	NNW
Rat	11 pm − 1 am	N
Ox	1 am − 3 am	NNE
Tiger	3 am − 5 am	ENE
Rabbit	5 am − 7 am	E

People who were born in the time of the dragon (7 a.m. to 9 a.m.), for example, should place their front door toward east-southeast.

5 *Qi* Locations Until 2043

Qi is as vital to the body as it is to a house or site because it represents energy and growth. Without *qi*, the land cannot sustain life and without *qi* a person will die. In addition, there is *sheng qi* and *si qi*: *sheng qi* is alive and generates energy; *si qi* is dead and stops growth. Where there is balance of the positive (*yang*) and negative (*yin*) forces, there is *sheng qi*; where there is imbalance there is *si qi*.

When people work and sleep in areas where there is an abundance of *sheng qi*, they are driven, energetic and innovative. Because of their enterprising attitudes and hard work they make a success out of everything they do, and are therefore more fortunate than others. Good *feng shui* does not guarantee that money drops from the sky or gold creeps under the door into the safe. Good *feng shui* provides the opportunity for a person to benefit from revitalising *qi* and make use of its energy to fulfil goals. In doing so, the person enjoys health and success.

The diagrams on the following pages, derived from the *Le Shu* theory of geomancy, outline plans of flats and houses and indicate *qi* locations from now to 2003, from 2004 to 2023, and from 2024 to 2043, which is the last year in a 60-year cycle. (After 2043, the *qi* locations will change again.) They are based on the *Le Shu* principle that there is *qi* in every room, building and site, and that within every flat or house, there are areas where *qi* is more vibrant than others. Even an area that is not vibrant with *qi* has *some qi*, and it is important to utilise it by placing the writing desk, bed or stove in its path.

Some people think that those who live in houses are more fortunate because they have more control over their environment and can alter it to suit their preferences and horoscopes. They can incorporate features to achieve balance of *yin* and *yang*, and they can make use of building form, space, structure, colour and other architectural elements to make their environments comfortable and aesthetically pleasing. Moreover, they have the opportunity to place their front door, master bedroom, living room and kitchen in the good *qi* areas.

I believe that people who live in high-rise flats are just as fortunate, even though they may have fewer options and more restrictions regarding the siting of their flats and the locations of their front doors and

31

bedrooms. They can still make the most of their situations by using the diagrams in this chapter to locate the *qi* areas, and by placing the important activities in those areas. Even a room with little *sheng qi* can be compensated for by good interior decoration and good sense of space and colour. It is important to realise that all *feng shui* defects can be rectified, and that all imbalances can be balanced.

The Le Shu *Grid*

How do we find the *qi* within any given room? Many geomancers draw the *Le Shu* grid on a plan of a proposed site, building or interior. The *Le Shu* grid is a simple drawing of nine squares. In the diagrams that follow, the grid has been drawn on different sites according to their relationship with the north point. To locate the *qi* on a proposed site, within a building, or within a room, find the diagram that is closest in orientation to what you are analysing. As you can see, the *qi* in some orientations changes every 20 years, while in others it remains consistent for a complete cycle of 60 years.

If you are building on a vacant piece of land, you can use the diagrams to place your proposed building on the *qi* area of the site. If you are analysing a proposed building, you can place your front door or master bedroom in the *qi* area indicated. And, if you are analysing an interior, use these diagrams to place your important furniture and activities in the *qi* areas.

The diagrams can also be used in conjunction with the year of birth chart in Chapter Four. The *Le Shu* grid tells you the location of the *qi*, while the year of birth chart provides favourable orientations for your front door and bed.

The red areas in the diagrams on pages 33-38 indicate the qi *locations for ▶ rooms, sites and buildings for three 20-year cycles.*

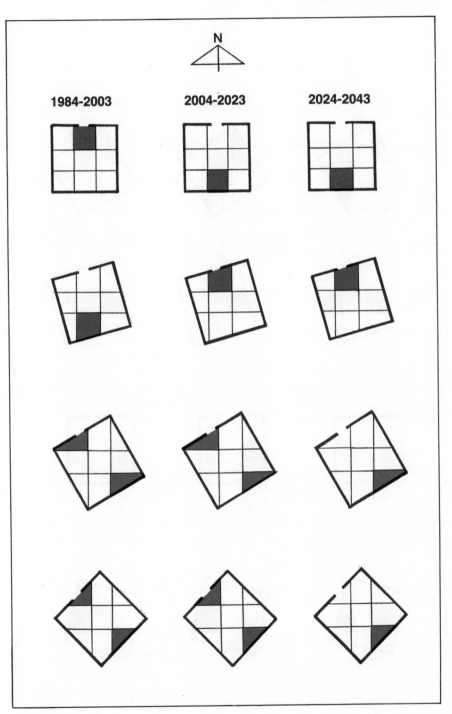

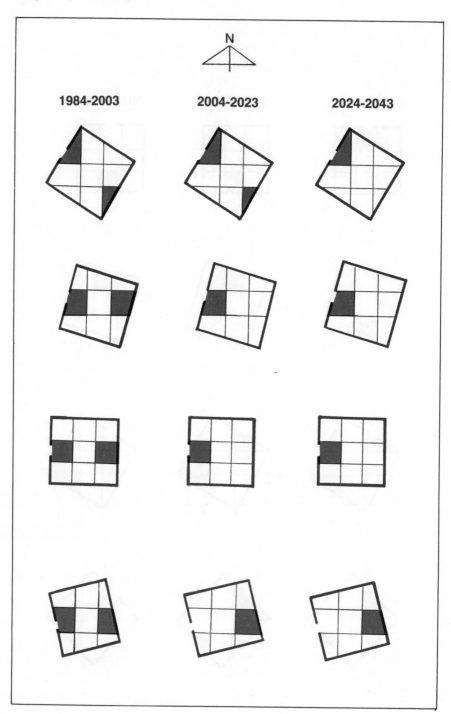

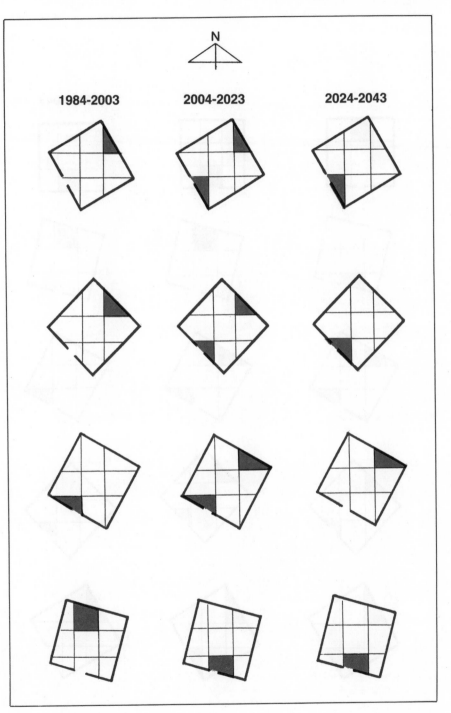

1984-2003 **2004-2023** **2024-2043**

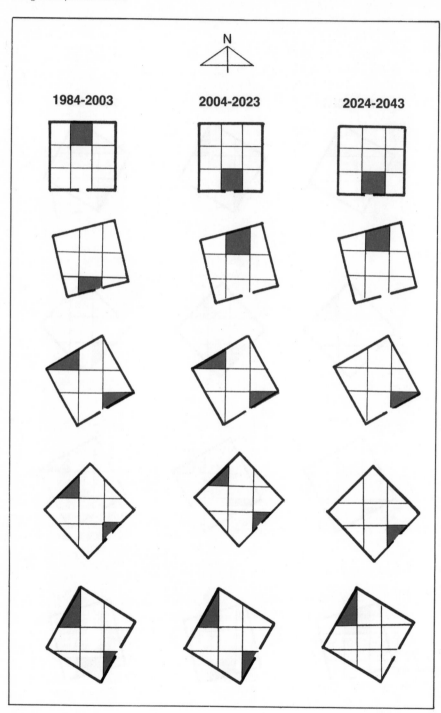

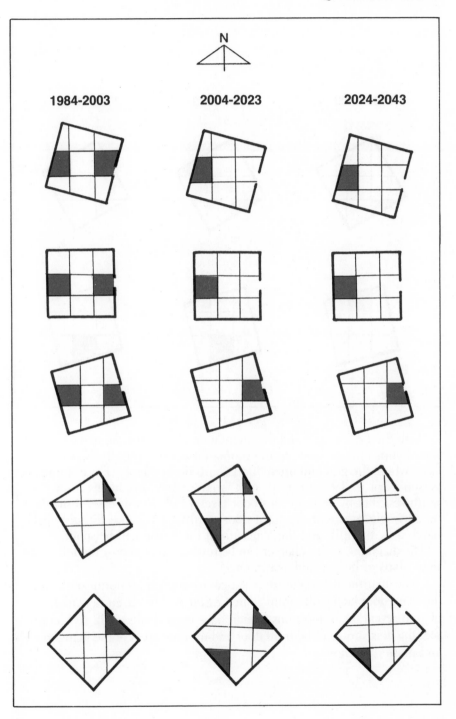

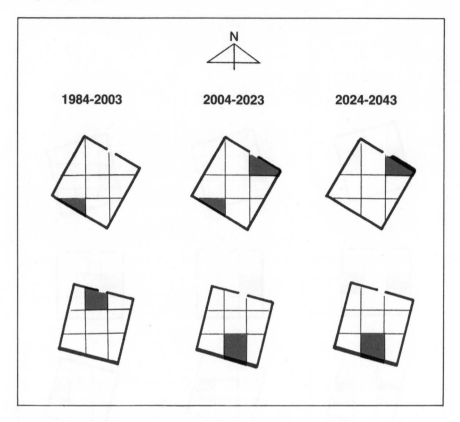

N

1984-2003   2004-2023   2024-2043

With the *Le Shu* grid and the orientation chart, you can make the best use of your interior space in the geomantic sense. Admittedly, there are cases where the grid and orientation charts do not apply. For example, a person born in 1940 or at 10 p.m. may wish to orient his front door northwest, but by doing so, his door faces a hill. In this case, it may not be advisable to orient the front door northwest because the *qi* will be blocked by the hill, and the *feng shui* of the house will be spoilt.

The diagrams in this chapter can be further explained by the following floor plans of houses and apartments.

The apartment at right, for instance, is oriented off north/south, with the main door facing off south. The *Le Shu* grid has been drawn on the plan to reveal the *qi* locations (which have been shaded red). As you can see, the *qi* is strong at the front door and in some areas of the living room and master bedroom.

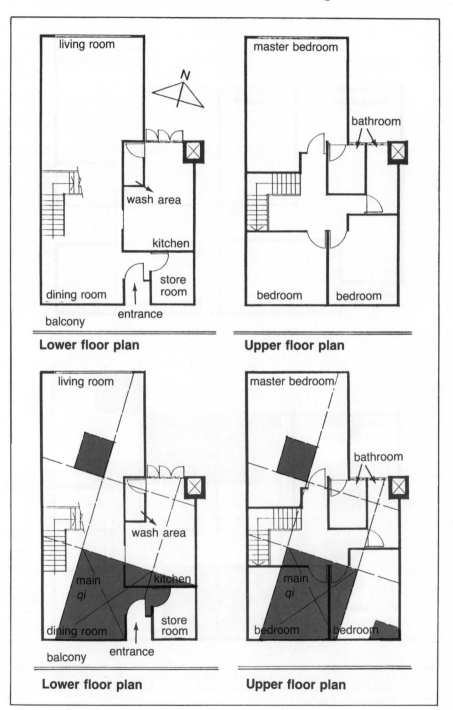

Lower floor plan

Upper floor plan

Lower floor plan

Upper floor plan

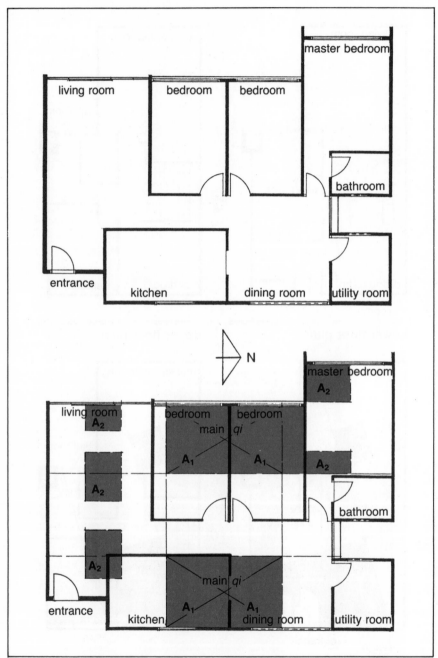

*The front door of this flat faces east. The qi (in red) is most abundant in the areas marked **A1** and less abundant in those marked **A2**. The best sitting areas in the living room are marked **A2**.*

A painting of a tiger is often displayed on a wall near the entrance of a home or business to dispel evil influences.

◀ *The Summer Palace was designed according to principles of balance, harmony and feng shui. The hill fronts a calm lake, the most important building is raised on a platform, and the other buildings form the shape of a horseshoe, a good luck symbol.*

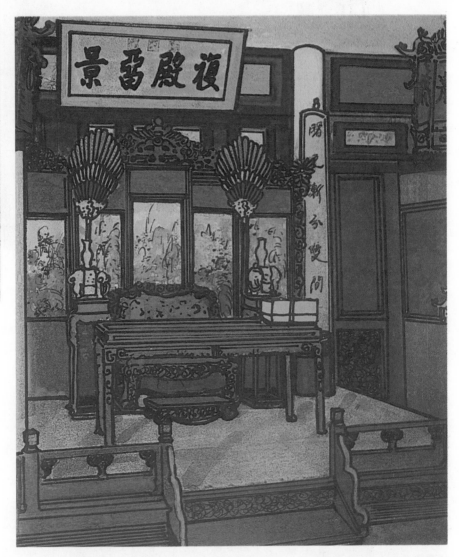

▲ *The imperial chair was designed according to feng shui principles. It was placed in front of a screen carved with favourable symbols and the backrest was constructed to give physical and symbolic protection to the emperor.*

◀ *This temple was closed. Could it have been affected by its position on a T-junction?*

This interior of the Dragon City restaurant in Singapore was designed according to feng shui *principles: red, the colour of happiness and auspiciousness, is used throughout; the front door is tilted to capture good feng shui; the fish tank is placed between two columns so they merge with the structure and do not act as a source of sha qi or imbalanced qi; and there is a pot of xian ren jang （仙人掌） near the back door, which faces a drain.*

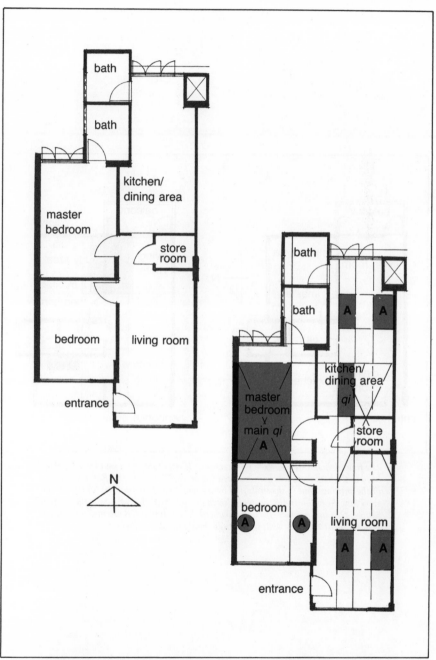

This apartment is oriented north/south with the front door facing west. The most important furniture — the beds, lounge chairs and study tables — should be placed in the locations marked A. The qi areas have been shaded red.

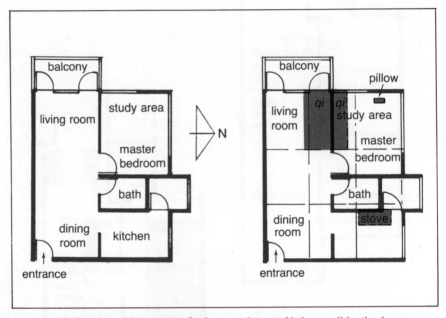

The front door of this two-room flat faces east. It is suitable for a small family whose head of the household was born between 5 a.m. and 7 a.m. In this flat, the qi is not at the entrance, but in the study and living areas. The best positions for the kitchen stove and the pillow in the master bedroom are indicated. By furnishing the flat in a simple, pleasant manner, the qi is enhanced. For a similar flat oriented west, the qi is found near the west wall, so the beds should be placed there.

6 Geomancy and Interior Elements

Building elements affect the internal environment and *feng shui* of a home or flat. The shape of a structure, for instance, can affect the space of the room and the flow of *qi*. Doors and windows admit *qi* and ventilation which sustain life. Passages and staircases carry *qi* from one space to another, from the lower level to the upper level and vice versa. It is important to design an interior to maximise the flow of *qi*.

Doors and Windows

The main door of a home or apartment is of vital importance because it breathes *qi* into the interior. If the main door is not oriented correctly, it can emit *si qi* or dead *qi*.

The gate, front door and back door should not be in line with one another or the luck of the home will be short-lived. According to the geomancer, *qi* travels from the front door to the back door in a straight line. If all the doors are in alignment, the *qi* becomes too vibrant. To retain the *qi* and make it less vibrant, a screen should be placed behind the front door or in front of the back door. Some geomancers hang a chime in the doorway to dispel the *sha qi* while others place a flute over the doors because in Cantonese, the word flute sounds like the word for disappear. Symbolically then, the flute makes the *sha qi* disappear.

The entrance hall should be located with reference to the *qi* of the interior space and in harmony with the horoscopic symbol of the owner of the property. The walls of the entry should not be too dark or too narrow or they will oppress the *qi* coming from the main door. And, psychologically, it is more pleasant to enter a home through a well-lit, well-proportioned doorway.

Windows should be located to capture fresh air and *qi*, and to shield the inhabitants from direct glare and heat.

Rooms

Even the shape or structure of a room has a significant effect on the *feng shui* of a house. Square, rectangular, and neat room shapes encourage the flow of *qi*, while irregular shapes suppress *qi*.

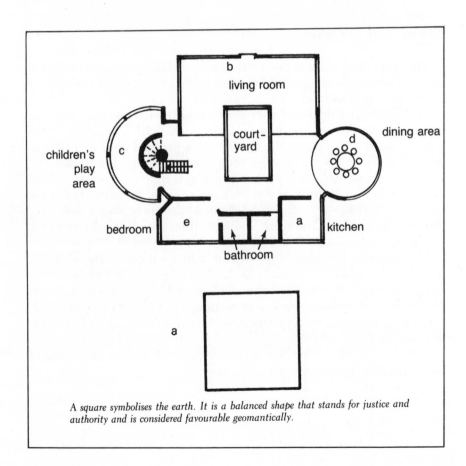

A *square symbolises the earth. It is a balanced shape that stands for justice and authority and is considered favourable geomantically.*

b

This shape is not practical according to the geomancer, because wind can get trapped in the internal court (marked x) and turbulent ill forces can gather there.

x

c

This is a fan shape that the geomancer classifies as bu jui qi（不聚气）, *which means "cannot keep* qi*."*

This symbol, chu long chu shui gc（猪笼出水格）, *is good because it stands for wealth and resembles the rattan cage of the pig, which allows water to flow in easily.*

d

e

This shape is neither auspicious nor inauspicious.

Walls, Ceilings, and Structural Beams and Columns

To the geomancer, walls have substantial influence on the *feng shui* of a house, apartment, or even a city. For example, the walls surrounding the Forbidden City give a sense of security to the inhabitants, and act as defensive elements, demarking boundaries and keeping evil spirits and earthly enemies from disturbing the people.

In interior spaces, walls are synonymous with the protective mountain ranges of a good *feng shui* site. Occupants should sit with their backs to solid walls to shield them from "danger," and so they can look out the window and capture a good view (especially of the sea, because water symbolises luck).

Solid walls are sometimes used to block off *sha qi,* and to deter the flow of *qi.* Houses in China are often planned so that the wall at the entrance deflects evil influences. On the other hand, walls must not block the flow of good *qi* from one space to another.

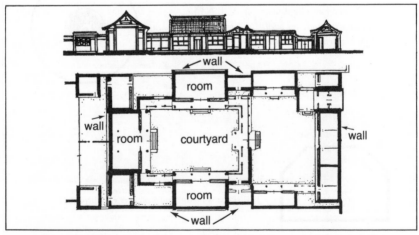

The walls of this courtyard house in Beijing enclose the compound, protect the privacy of the tenants and prevent dust carried by northerly winds to enter the house.

Before the walls, ceilings and floor elements are incorporated into the plan of a room, it is wise to measure their height, breadth and width to ensure that they are of good geomantic dimensions. (See Chapter Four for information on good and bad dimensions.)

Although it is normal practice to design rooms for the purpose of a certain activity, changes in family, ways of living, and in the location of *qi* during the family cycle may require structural alterations. It may be advisable therefore, to design an interior so it is versatile enough to meet these changes. Some geomancers recommend that internal partitions be demountable and erectable so the interior space can be rearranged as desired.

In terms of ceilings, geomancers believe that beams and rafters should neither be exposed nor built over a sleeping area. Sloping ceilings are also unlucky because they oppress or deter the flow of *qi*. If a beam looks oppressive, hang a chime on it to break the *sha qi*.

The geomancer believes it is bad feng shui to sit under a heavy beam all the time.

Structural columns should be placed at the four corners of the room or within the walls to prevent the disruption of *qi*. If there is an exposed column within an interior, it creates *sha qi* or an imbalance of *qi*, so a person should not sit with his back to it. By putting a solid wall between the column and the person, the wall will block the unbalanced *qi* and provide protection.

Staircases

The staircase and connecting corridors are important elements in the layout of an interior. To the geomancer, a staircase that fronts the main door and runs in a straight flight from one floor to another is a source of *sha qi*. It is also not wise to place the staircase at the centre of the house.

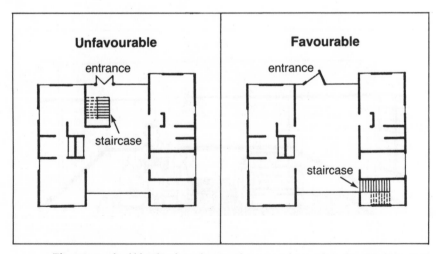

The staircase should be placed at a location that cannot be seen from the entrance area.

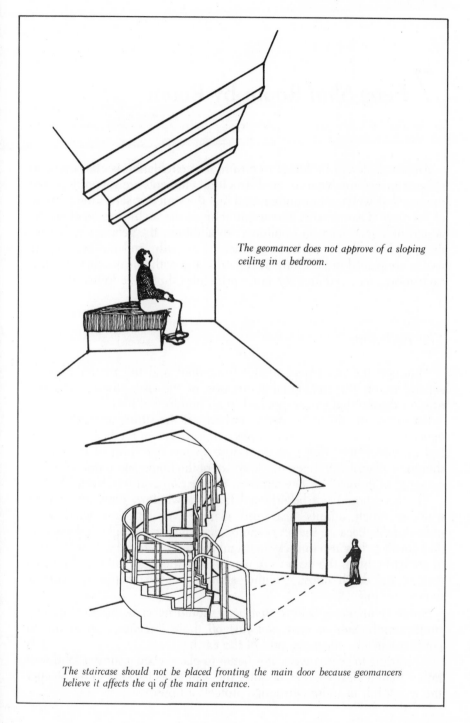

The geomancer does not approve of a sloping ceiling in a bedroom.

The staircase should not be placed fronting the main door because geomancers believe it affects the qi of the main entrance.

7 *Feng Shui* Room by Room

Architects design buildings to ensure that circulation is efficient, that interior spaces are dynamic, that structural elements are supportive, that rooms relate well to one another, and that the structure serves the purpose of the user. Geomancers also try to achieve the architect's goals in the design of a good *feng shui* building. In addition, the geomancer locates the *qi*, places the important activities in its path, and makes sure the rooms are placed in harmony with nature and with one another. Within each room, too, certain geomantic principles should be followed.

The Bedroom

Although the placement of the front door and the master's bed is dependent on the individual horoscope of the user, there are some rules-of-thumb that can be applied to all homes and flats.

Bedrooms should be located anywhere off the sitting area, or at the upper level. The most important piece of furniture in the bedroom is the bed on which the master of the house spends one-third of his life. It should be placed with reference to the *qi* of the home and room. (See the drawings of *qi* locations devised from the *Le Shu* grid in Chapter Five.)

The bed should not be oriented facing a window, especially a west window which admits heat and glare. Even an east window is unfavourable because the users can be disturbed by sunlight and glare in the morning. It is also unlucky to orient the bed towards the door because in ancient China, the dead were placed with their feet towards the front door of the death house. Neither should the bed be placed under a sloping ceiling.

Some geomancers believe that beds should never be oriented exactly north, south, east or west, but *just off* those directions, so as not to conflict with the magnetic pull of the earth.

According to geomancers, it is better to place a bed against a solid wall rather than a glass window because the wall gives backing to the sleeper the way a hill or mountain range protects a house.

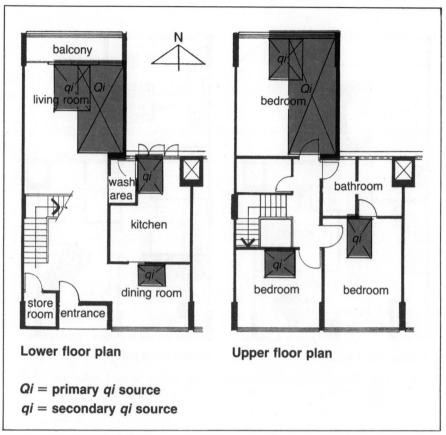

This plan shows a house and its primary and secondary qi *areas. The important activities should be placed in the red* qi *areas, as shown in the next diagram.*

The bed should not be placed facing a mirror. The Chinese believe that the soul leaves the body when a person sleeps. If there is a mirror just opposite the bed, the soul may get a shock on seeing its image, and this, in turn, can disturb the spirit of the person. Mirrors can be used in other rooms or narrow corridors however, to give the illusion of spaciousness and to deflect and stimulate the flow of *qi*.

The dressing table in a bedroom should not be placed opposite a window because glare will be reflected in the glass or mirror. And, furniture placed outside the door of a bedroom should not be arranged in the shape of a bow which points into the room. If this happens, the health of the person using the bedroom may be affected.

Lower floor plan   **Upper floor plan**

The seats in the living room, the study tables, sink, dining table and beds have been placed in the qi *areas. The beds have each been oriented according to the horoscopes of the users.*

The Kitchen

The *yin-yang* theory of balance should be applied to the design of a kitchen. The sink or refrigerator should not be next to the stove, or there could be a conflict between the water (*yin*) and fire (*yang*) elements.

The stove should be placed according to the horoscope of the homeowner, but generally, the stove should face south or east because it belongs to the fire element. In any case, it should not be placed in a dead corner where there is insufficient lighting and ventilation. The kitchen should not be in front of or next to a toilet because the geomancer believes the two rooms are incompatible.

Kitchens of coffee houses and restaurants should not be placed in the south or east because the kitchen belongs to the fire element and will clash with the fire element in the east and melt the gold element in the south. (This could mean that the restaurant owner will not be successful.)

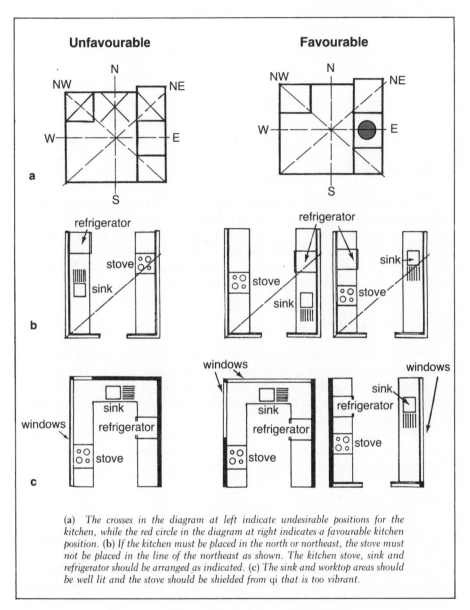

(a) *The crosses in the diagram at left indicate undesirable positions for the kitchen, while the red circle in the diagram at right indicates a favourable kitchen position.* (b) *If the kitchen must be placed in the north or northeast, the stove must not be placed in the line of the northeast as shown. The kitchen stove, sink and refrigerator should be arranged as indicated.* (c) *The sink and worktop areas should be well lit and the stove should be shielded from* qi *that is too vibrant.*

Most geomancers do not like to place the kitchen in the north, northeast, or northwest. They consider the north direction as the door to the spiritual way, the northeast as the door to evil, and the northwest as impractical (possibly because the wind from Mongolia brought yellow dust to the northern parts of China).

The Living Room

The Chinese believe it is not good *feng shui* to arrange the lounge seats in the living room so they resemble a bow or a triangle and point at the bedroom. Symbolically, the bow can shoot an arrow at the person sleeping in the bed. It is also unfavourable to place the master's chair facing a large door or window, because when he reads, he will suffer from glare. To the geomancer, glare is *sha qi*.

The Dining Room

According to the Chinese, the dining table should be round because the circle symbolises heavenly blessings. (A square symbolises earth, which is inferior to heaven.) The table should be placed under balanced lighting in the centre of the room so the diners can benefit from good ventilation.

Dining chairs must be in pairs of four, six or eight because the Chinese believe that luck comes in even numbers and that a single number represents loneliness.

The Study

The shape and placement of furniture in the study area is important. The master's and children's study tables should be rectangular, and placed in the *qi* area (according to the *Le Shu* grid and the horoscopes of the users). They should be placed against a solid wall for backing, with the window preferably at the left, to provide a view and adequate ventilation.

The size of the writing desk should be in accordance with the auspicious measurements of the geomancer's ruler. (See Chapter Four.)

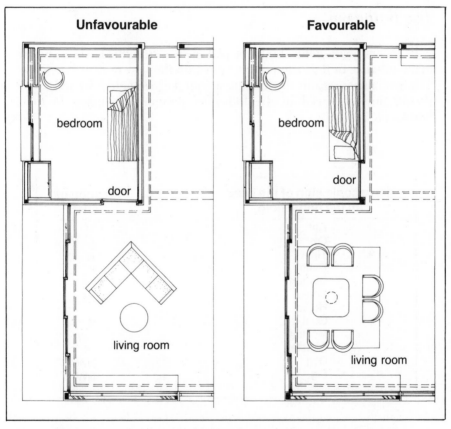

The furniture in the living room should not be arranged so it points at the door of the bedroom, and the bed should not be placed so the sleeper's feet face the door. The plan on the right is more favourable according to the geomancer.

The Bathroom

In general, bathrooms should be placed away from the kitchen and the main entrance or they can pollute or disturb the flow of *qi* in the house. The geomancer regards the toilet as a poor *feng shui* element and says it should not be placed in the following positions according to these horoscopic symbols:

Horoscopic sign of the head of the household	Position of toilet
Rat	N
Ox	N
Tiger	N
Rabbit	E
Dragon	SE
Snake	SE
Horse	S
Goat	S
Monkey	SW
Rooster	W
Dog	NW
Pig	NW

The drawings that follow illustrate many of the *feng shui* principles described on the preceding pages.

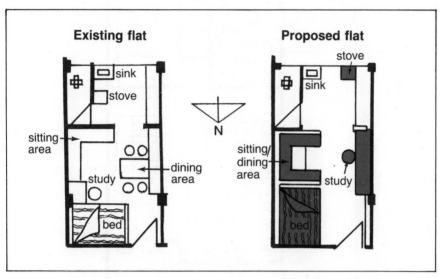

This bed-sitter flat was studied to see if its feng shui *could be improved. The owner of the flat was born in 1936 during the time of the rat (11 p.m. and 1 a.m.), so his favourable orientation is north. His furniture has not been placed to make the most of* feng shui. *His bed, for example, is oriented west. It should be facing north, as shown in the proposed plan. The study is in a dark, poorly ventilated area and should be placed along the west wall. (Notice how one wall of the kitchen can be reduced to allow light from the back of the flat to reach the centre of the room.) With the right choice of furniture, the sitting area can be designed to act as a sitting and dining area. The kitchen stove should have a southern orientation, as indicated.*

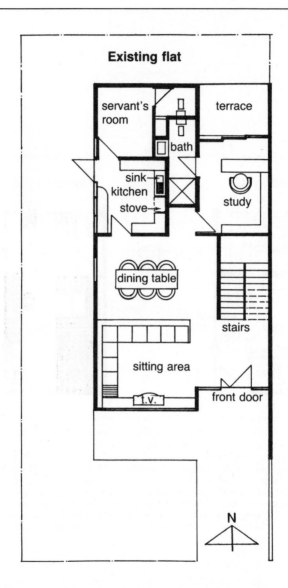

Existing flat

servant's room

terrace

bath

sink
kitchen
stove

study

dining table

stairs

sitting area

t.v.

front door

N

This semi-detached house is owned by a man born during the time of the horse (11 a.m. to 1 p.m.). According to the geomancer, his favourable orientation is south. Although the feng shui of the house is relatively good, there are several shortcomings: (1) the staircase faces the front door; (2) the study table faces the window; (3) the servant's room is insufficiently lit and poorly ventilated; (4) the kitchen stove is placed in the wrong position and is too near the sink; (5) the dining table is rectangular and the dining area is badly lit; (6) the television set is placed against the windows, which makes for difficult viewing.

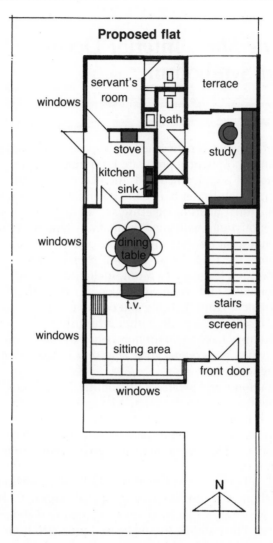

Proposed flat

servant's room

windows

terrace

bath

stove

study

kitchen

sink

windows

dining table

t.v.

stairs

screen

windows

sitting area

front door

windows

N

To improve the feng shui *of the house within a limited budget, the following minor alterations should be made: (1) a screen should be placed at the entrance to eliminate the* sha qi *of the staircase; (2) the study table should be re-oriented so the light source comes from the left; (3) windows should be added in the servant's room for better lighting and to encourage cross ventilation (both of which promote the flow of* qi*); (4) the stove should be moved away from the sink so it faces south; (5) a circular dining table should replace the rectangular one and windows should be added to brighten up the dining area; (6) windows should also be added in the living room to encourage cross ventilation, and the television set should be placed away from the windows. Upstairs, the master bedroom should be placed above the living room and the bed should face south.*

8 *Feng Shui*, Interior Decor and Symbolism

An interior designer is concerned with space, light, and colour in the creation of an atmosphere appropriate for dining, sleeping and working. A *feng shui* expert is concerned with the placement of furniture and the location of *qi*, which can enhance the potential of the occupants. These seemingly dissimilar areas of expertise are, in fact, closely linked. Good *feng shui* is synonymous with good ventilation, appropriate lighting, good proportion, and most importantly, a sense of balance. And good interior design enhances the *feng shui* of a room, shop or office.

The architectural features of a room, including structural walls, ceiling and floor elements, and windows and doors, affect the flow of *qi* in a house or apartment. And, lighting and colour certainly play a role in the quality of *qi* in a room. A room with few furnishings but a balanced and tranquil layout may have a vibrant flow of *qi* that can be rejuvenating and health preserving. Very often, good *feng shui* is both good architecture and good interior design.

Qi, the vital force and breath of life, animates all things, but it should be complemented by good design elements to reach its potential. Although each home has a unique *feng shui* situation and interior style, there are some basic design concepts that should be applied to all interiors to create a comfortable environment and make maximum use of invisible revitalising forces.

In general, a house or apartment should have a functional plan with good circulation and an interesting spatial concept. It should be aesthetically pleasing, with a good sense of proportion and an appropriate colour scheme. The building should be well-protected from weather, and radiation from the sun should be minimalised. Ventilation is also very important. *Qi* should flow through the body the way fresh air flows through the house; and *si qi* is synonymous with stagnant, damp air.

Furniture

Furniture should be placed in the *qi* areas, within the path of fresh air, and under adequate lighting. It should be harmonious with the other interior elements and arranged in a balanced manner. (Much of the theory of *feng shui*, you will recall, is based on the *yin-yang* principle of balance and harmony.)

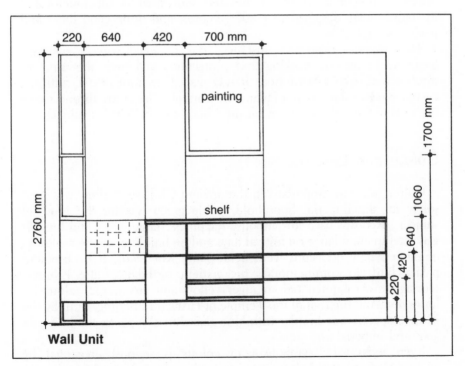

The size of every piece of furniture is significant to the geomancer. Each piece of this wall unit is of favourable geomantic measurement.

The Chinese, who are fond of the language of symbols, often furnish their homes symbolically. They'll have a chair in the shape of a tortoise, which represents longevity, or a round dining table, which symbolises heavenly blessings.

Furniture design has always been a concern of the Chinese, even thousands of years ago. The emperors in ancient times spent fortunes on the interior decoration and furnishing of their imperial palaces. Dragons, phoenixes and many good luck symbols were intricately carved into screens and various pieces of furniture to promote good *feng shui*. The chairs, writing desks, beds, couches and stools used by the emperor and his family were designed to render comfort and bring good luck, and placed to capture *qi*.

The imperial chair, for instance, was designed with a generous backrest, to provide backing and protection, and with the armrests outstretched, like a horseshoe. It was placed in front of a beautifully carved screen inlaid with a favourable symbol. The entire throne rested on a platform so the emperor sat on a higher level than his subjects.

Colour and Lighting

Colour was also important to the ancient Chinese. Yellow was used solely for the imperial household, while green was for the imperial subjects. Red was used to symbolise happiness, fame, glory and luck. It was used in abundance on festival days and on buildings where weddings or other happy occasions were held. *Yang Xin Dian*, the retirement palace built to commemorate the sixtieth birthday of the Empress Dowager, was painted red, orange, yellow and green, the colour for longevity. And the roof of the Temple of Heaven in Beijing, built by the Ming emperor, was circular with blue glazed tiles to please the heavenly gods and imperial ancestors.

Even today, the symbolism of colour is seriously regarded by geomancers: red stands for auspiciousness; green is longevity; yellow is authority; blue is heavenly blessings; and white is purity.

The colour schemes of wall finishes can make a room warmer or cooler, and can affect the *feng shui* of the interior. If the user of the space is of the fire element and the room he works in all day is painted red or another warm colour (also of the fire element), the elements can clash. On the other hand, if the user is of the water element and works in a warm-coloured room, the fire element cools the water element, thus creating a more balanced situation.

Light enables colour and forms to be seen. As with furniture, light and colour should not be a source of imbalance or *sha qi*. To the geomancer, glare is considered *sha qi* and an irritation to the users of the space. Direct glare from lamps should be avoided by using appropriate shading devices.

Reflective surfaces are sometimes placed on walls to add light to a room and to give the illusion of spaciousness. Geomancers use mirrors to deter evil influence and to draw in good *qi*.

Paintings

The Chinese believe that balance is the essence of good design. Even ornaments, paintings, calligraphy and decorative motifs on the walls of Chinese homes and shops are hung in balanced pairs, because happiness is said to come in two's. It is common to see the characters 囍囍 (*xi xi* or "double happiness") on a prominent wall of a wedding reception.

In the home, the length and width of a pair of painted scrolls hung on a wall should be the same. If works of art are framed, they should be in the auspicious shapes of the fan or circle. The paintings should depict scenic landscapes, plants that symbolise good fortune, or figures of important deities who have the power to control evil spirits.

A good scenic landscape painting depicts the balance of the *yin* and *yang* forces in the natural environment. Solid, rugged rocks and mountain ranges contrast the slow-moving water courses and the white clouds. Paintings of plants and flowers that represent good fortune and endurance (including the bamboo and the chrysanthemum), and legendary figures (like *Shen Shu* and *Yu Lei*) are often found on the doors of important buildings and temples to repel evil influences.

一九八四年六月廿一日

夢霞

Patterns

Patterns on walls, floors and ceilings are also symbolic. For instance, patterns that resemble the tortoise shell represent longevity; clouds symbolise wisdom; coins stand for prosperity; and fish for success. Chinese characters — like 人 (*ren*), 口 (*kou*), and 丁 (*ding*), which are favourable symbols for future generations — are often incorporated in floor patterns to enhance the *feng shui* of an interior.

These characters, plants, animals and other auspicious symbols can be used as patterns on furniture and decorative interior elements like carpets, draperies, and tiles to bring good fortune.

Pattern	Significance
elephant	wisdom
pine tree	longevity and endurance
vase	peace
phoenix and dragon	perfect balance of *yin* and *yang*
fish scale	success
lotus	endurance and uprightness
water ripples	wealth and heavenly blessing
clouds	heavenly blessing and wisdom
gold pieces	wealth
chi ling	wisdom
yin yang (birds)	union of man and woman
flowers	wealth
tortoise shell	longevity
eight symbols of eight immortals	longevity
old coins	wealth
bats	luck
cranes	fidelity, honesty and longevity
deer	wealth

◄ *In a Chinese painting, the black painted area* (yang) *and the empty space* (yin) *must balance. Even the unpainted space is part of the composition.*

Chinese character	Hanyu Pinyin	Symbolic equivalent	Significance
鵲	*xi*	bird	double happiness
蝠	*fu*	bat	luck
寿	*shou*	old man (*shou xing*)	longevity
吉	*ji*	fruit	luck
如	*ru*	fish	success
祝	*zhu*	bamboo	good wishes

The symbol of the Eight Trigrams — an eight-sided plate with ancient numerical symbols — is often used to deflect evil influences. The Trigrams are associated with the ancient divination based on the Yi-Jing.

a

b

c

(a) *The mythological chimera represents power and dignity and is usually found on embroidered pillowcases or mats, or sculpted in porcelain.*

(b) *The phoenix, which symbolises grace and wisdom, is often found on ceiling panels, screens, carpets, pillowcases, mats and wall murals.*

(c) *The deer, which signifies luck and wealth, is often used on decorative wall hangings.*

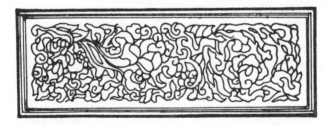

These patterns, derived from the chrysanthemum and other enduring plants, symbolise both longevity and patience. They can be incorporated in wall paper, carpeting, floor tiles, ceiling decoration, and table and bed linens.

These patterns, derived from the shape of the tortoise shell, symbolise longevity.

The water and cloud pattern symbolises heavenly blessings.

Plants and Fish Tanks

In Chinese dwellings, plants that can survive harsh weather are often placed around the home as symbols of longevity. Chrysanthemum, pines, plums, bamboo and even cactus are more common than roses or other flowers that bloom and die quickly.

People often put fish tanks in their homes to symbolise good fortune. Geomancers believe that fish tanks are especially auspicious if the owner is of the fire element because the fire will be balanced by the water. Geomancers often tell their clients to place a fish tank in their homes or offices to absorb evil influences.

Sculpture

Animals that symbolise strength and power are often sculpted or cast in porcelain or bronze and placed around the house to repel evil spirits. Popular animals taken from nature like the lion, tiger, and elephant, and mythological creatures like the chimera and the unicorn are often used. The dragon, the most powerful of the animal symbols, was often placed around the imperial palaces as a symbol of strength.

Animals like the tortoise that are known to have long lives are used to symbolise longevity. And, sculptures of fish can be found in many homes because the Chinese word for fish sounds like the word for success or abundance.

9 *Feng Shui* for the Office and Shophouse

There are many similarities between geomantic doctrine for the home and the office. The basic rules of geomancy concerning the surrounding environment, the location of *qi*, and the orientation of the main doors also apply to offices and shophouses. Some geomancers use the following guidelines when recommending orientations for businesses:

Business/firm/shop	Favourable orientation for the front door
law firm, medical centre, shipping firm	north or east
accounting firm, finance company, bank, architectural firm	northwest or southeast
import/export company, trading company	north or east
provision shop, saloon	north or southeast

As with the completion date of a house, the selection of an auspicious date for the official opening of a business must be found in the *Tong Shu*, the Chinese almanac. The Chinese believe that the *Tong Shu*, written centuries ago and revised in the early 1900's, was based on information derived from the positions of constellations. The almanac relates the constellations to the horoscopic symbols which are associated with the geomancer's compass.

The Importance of Addresses

The address number of an office or shophouse is significant in the eyes of the geomancer. The numbers 2, 5, 6, 8, 9 and 10 are lucky: 2 means easy, 5 means in harmony with the Five Elements, 6 represents wealth, 8 means becoming rich, 9 is synonymous with longevity, and 10 means sure. Thus, an office address like 289 means "easy to become rich for a long period," or that the business will prosper for a long time. On the other hand, the number 744 means "sure to die," or that the business will not succeed. The number 4 is unpopular because in Cantonese it sounds like the word *si* meaning to die. The number 1 is also not very popular, although it is not necessarily unlucky.

The Chinese always prefer to use numbers in double digits because this represents a duality and, therefore, avoids the feeling of loneliness. Number 3 is not particularly lucky even though it sounds like the word "alive" in Cantonese. Some people do prefer to use it however, as in 7373, which means "sure to live on."

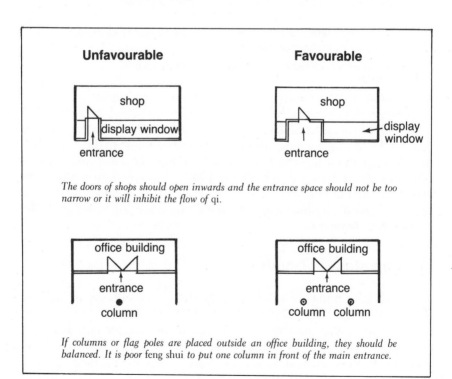

The doors of shops should open inwards and the entrance space should not be too narrow or it will inhibit the flow of qi.

If columns or flag poles are placed outside an office building, they should be balanced. It is poor feng shui to put one column in front of the main entrance.

The Signficance of Shop Names

The placement and significance of sign boards and the names of shops are important. Sign boards must be installed at an auspicious moment that is in harmony with the horoscope of the shopowner.

The name of the shop should convey good luck, wealth and success. Some of the common names for shops are: *Xing Li* （顺利） which means "smooth success," *Fa Da* （发达） or "prosperity and success," *Guang Li* （广利） or "great success," *Guang Yi* （广益） or "great benefit," and *Ji Chang* （吉祥） or "good luck." On the other hand, if the name of the shop means poor luck, the business may not prosper. A shop with the name *Wu Li* （无利） or "no profit" is expected to close down.

Some geomancers use the Five Element precepts to create an appropriate name for a shop. The chart that follows gives some common words and their associations with the Five Elements:

Water（水）	**Fire** （火）	**Wood**（木）	**Gold** （金）	**Earth**（土）
Fu （富）	*Du* （度）	*Gui* （贵）	*Shang* （商）	*Yin* （营）
Wang（凰）	*Tang*（堂）	*Guan* （关）	*Sheng*（生）	*Yu* （宇）
Hong （红）	*Le* （乐）	*Guang*（广）	*Si* （司）	*An* （安）
Fu （福）	*Jing* （金）	*Gong* （宫）	*Xia* （厦）	*Wu* （无）
Bi （壁）	*Dian*（店）	*Kong* （孔）	*Chang*（厂）	*Wang*（望）

When the Five Elements (and the words that are associated with them) are matched in the following combinations on the signs of shophouses they have both good and bad connotations. These combinations are favourable:

> water + wood (wood grows with the nourishment of water)
> wood + fire (fire becomes stronger with the addition of wood)
> fire + earth (earth is purified by fire)
> earth + gold (gold is protected by earth)
> gold + water (gold enriches water)

These combinations are unfavourable:

water + fire (water puts out fire)
fire + gold (gold is weakened by fire)
gold + wood (wood is incompatible with gold)
wood + earth (wood can be covered by earth)
earth + water (water is lost in the earth)

Some geomancers prefer shop names made up of Chinese characters that have a certain number of strokes. A character made up of an odd number of strokes is *yang* and a character with an even number of strokes is *yin*. The character — (*yi*) for example is *yang*, and 二 (*er*) is *yin*. Shop names with characters of odd/even (*yang/yin*) number sequences are considered favourable as are those with *yin/yang*, *yin/yin/yang*, and *yin/yang/yang* sequences. Unfavourable sequences include: *yin/yang/yin* and *yang/yin/yang*.

Feng Shui *and Office Design*

Some geomancers think an office at the end of a central corridor is unlucky because the *sha qi* from the hall can exert an unfavourable influence on the tenants. The doors of an office placed at the dead end of a long hallway should be shifted away from the corridor to avoid *sha qi*. In some offices, the entrance is shielded by a screen so that *sha qi* is deflected and cannot flow directly into the interior. This technique is also used in Beijing houses.

The manager's work-table and the accountant's safe are the most important office furniture. They should be placed with reference to the horoscope of the managing director. The desk should be of favourable measurements. In some firms, the legs of the desk are screwed into the floor so it cannot be shifted away from the luck.

It is poor *feng shui* and bad interior design to place the desk facing a window because the glare from outside will strain the eyes. Radiation from the sun may be even more intense just next to the window. It is also bad practice to place the manager's table and chair in front of a large window. On a bright day, the client may have difficulty looking at the manager because of glare, and the manager's face may be in the shade.

If window curtains are necessary, patterns of bamboo, chrysanthemum and good luck characters should be used. Some geomancers suggest placing pots of bamboo or chrysanthemum, sculptures of horses (symbolising efficiency and vitality) and tortoises (for longevity), tanks of gold fish, and flutes at strategic office locations to eliminate *si qi* and enhance *sheng qi*.

Office lighting should be evenly distributed to achieve balance and efficiency. Natural ventilation is preferable to air-conditioning because good cross breezes eliminate *si qi*. Care must be taken to ensure even distribution of air so the office workers do not suffer from cold draughts which can make them ill and disturb the balance of *qi*.

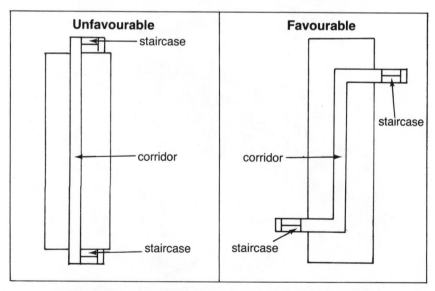

It is bad feng shui *practice to place staircases, lifts, toilets and doors at the end of a long corridor in an office building.*

The interior of an office should be designed or arranged so the manager sits with his back against a solid partition. This provides backing the way a hill protects a house or a mountain range protects a city. Other partitions throughout the office should be well placed so the flow of *qi* is not disrupted. For instance, a solid partition should not be placed so it disrupts a view of the sea.

According to some geomancers, lifts that rumble and are painted black are not good *feng shui*. Fountains outside businesses must be placed with reference to the *qi* orientation and the water should spray at a height which is geomantically favourable.

The office or shophouse should be built in harmony with the surrounding structures. Is this the way to achieve harmony?

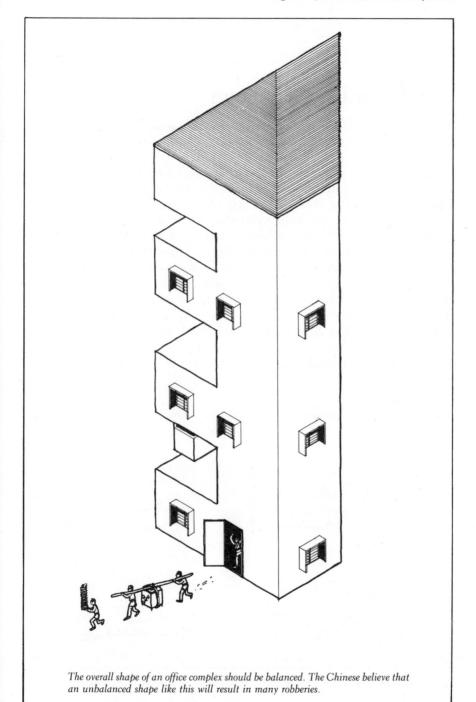

The overall shape of an office complex should be balanced. The Chinese believe that an unbalanced shape like this will result in many robberies.

10 Garden Geomancy

The philosophy of *yin* and *yang* is evident in Chinese garden design. A feeling of balance and continuity is created by the garden walls which link various elements like the rocks, trees, plants and bridges. Square and round openings in the walls symbolise earth and heaven, and the pavilions, bridges and paths are built in accordance with *feng shui* beliefs.

Bridges and paths in particular are often constructed in zigzag patterns to avoid *sha qi* and evil influences. This is done because the geomancer believes that good *qi* travels along meandering lines and *sha qi* along straight lines. The Chinese believe that roads or rivers that run in straight lines may bring destruction, while meandering lines follow the path of nature, and therefore comply with Taoist philosophy of garden design. (Although the Chinese base their architectural concepts on the Confucian idea of formality and symmetry, they follow Taoist doctrine in the garden.)

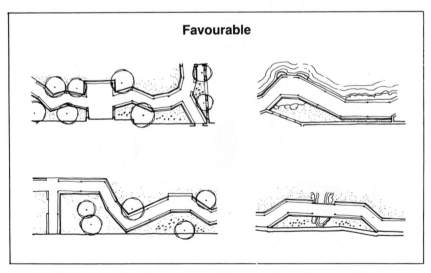

Favourable

Chinese garden paths (and interior corridors) should be winding to avoid sha qi.

The pebble mosaics in the Chinese garden are designed to emphasise the alternations and duality of *yin* and *yang*. And, statues of symbolic animals such as the tortoise, deer, dragon, lion and crane are often placed at strategic positions to enhance the garden and bring good luck.

The four sides of a garden are associated with four mythical animals: east with the azure dragon; south with the red phoenix, west with the white tiger; and north with the black tortoise. A stream, symbolising wealth, is usually built to the east of the garden, while a manmade lake is

Walls, trees, stones, plants, manmade hills and pavilions work together in the garden to enhance feng shui.

ideal on the south end. Meandering paths leading to pavilions are best at the west, and the north should be protected by manmade rockery complete with waterfalls.

In large gardens, pagodas are placed in the northeast or southwest directions (the doors of the devil) to repel evil influences. In smaller gardens, miniature porcelain pagodas are used and incorporated into the rockeries, and miniature mountains are constructed to act as protective hills.

Pavilions are often constructed in one of the following shapes: the square, which symbolises the earth; a five-sided figure, which is associated with the Five Elements; a six-sided figure, which symbolises wealth; or an eight-sided figure, which symbolises prosperity.

If manmade lakes and ponds are used, they should not be constructed in rigid geometric shapes like squares or rectangles. Their banks should be made to look as natural as possible and water lillies should be planted in the water to represent uprightness and to protect the garden against evil influences. Live tortoises and goldfish should be kept for good luck.

The planting of trees is also carefully considered. Trees that symbolise longevity like the pine, willow, and cypress are often used. In China, Wu Tong trees (aleurites cordata) are often planted in gardens because they do not collapse easily. Flowers, too, should be selected for their longevity. The chrysanthemum, orchid, plum and other enduring plants are suitable.

A Chinese garden is considered beautiful when rough textures contrast with smooth, and still rocks balance with flowing streams. For this reason, *Yuan Ye* (园艺) , the Chinese garden manual, suggests that the best site for a garden is on the edge of a lake with a view of the mountains. In such cases, *qi* is indeed in accordance with the vital spirit of nature.

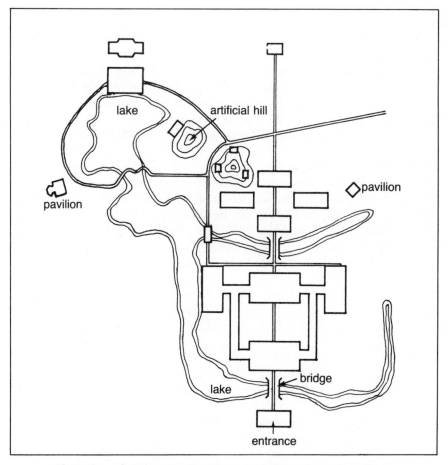

This garden, called Cheng Du Chow Tang, *was built by a famous Tang dynasty poet. The complex walls were designed so a manmade lake could pass through the main gate. The northern (back) portion of the garden was slightly higher than the front and the bridge across the lake zigzagged to avoid* sha qi. *Artificial hills were also built to create a favourable landscape.*

References in Chinese

Ceng Zi Nan 曾子南 , *San Yuan Di Li Tu Wen Jian Gie* 三元地理图文浅解, Taipei 台北, 1965

Cheng Jia Cheng 清家请, *Jia Zai Feng Shui* 家宅风水, n.d.

Feng Shui Guai Tan 风水怪谈, 1963.

Gu Zin Tu Shu Zhi Cheng 古今图书集成, China 中国, 1726.

Hsiao Zhi 肃吉, *Wu Xing Da Yi* 五行大义, China 中国, 600 A.D.

Jiang Ping Jie 蒋平楷, *Di Li Zheng Shu* 地理正疏, Taiwan 台湾, 1980.

Luo Jin Chang Jie 罗经详解, Taiwan 台湾, n.d.

Nan Hai Guan 南海关, *Kanyu Xue Yuan Li* 堪舆学原理, Hong Kong 香港, 1971.

Shui Long Jing 水龙经, n.d.

Tian Gong Kai Wu 天工开物, China 中国, 1637 A.D.

Wang Chao Chuan 黄朝全, *Kanyu Ao Mi* 堪舆奥秘, Taiwan 台湾, 1980.

Wang Qi Yan 王启燊, *Di Lin Ren Jie* 地灵人杰, Taipei 台北, 1978.

Xie Yi Xian 谢易显, *Shu Shu Zhi Ke Xue* 术娄之科学, Hong Kong 香港, 1978.

Xie Yi Xian 谢易显, *Yi Shu Xian Yi* 易术显义, Hong Kong 香港, 1978.

References in English

Ball, Dyer, *Things Chinese*, London, 1904.

Bring, Mitchell, and Josse Wayembergh, *Japanese Garden Design and Meaning*, New York, 1981.

De Groot, J. J. M., *The Religious System of China*, Leyden, 1892.

Dore, Henry, *Research into Chinese Superstitions*, Vol. 4, Shanghai, 1928.

Eitel, E. J., *Feng Shui, or the Rudiments of Natural Science in China*, Hong Kong, 1873.

Forlag, G., *Chinese Buddhist Monasteries*, London, 1937.

Graham, David, *Folk Religion in S. W. China*, Washington, 1961.

Lip, Evelyn, *Chinese Beliefs and Superstitions*, Singapore, 1985.

_____ , *Chinese Geomancy*, Singapore, 1979.

_____ , *Chinese Temples and Deities*, Singapore, 1981.

_____ , *Chinese Temple Architecture in Singapore*, Singapore, 1983.

_____ , "Feng Shui, Chinese Colours and Symbolism", *Singapore Institute of Architects Journal*, Singapore, July, 1978.

_____ , "Geomancy and Building", *Development and Construction*, Singapore, 1977.

Needham, Joseph, *Science and Civilization in China*, London, 1982.

Skinner, Stephen, *The Living Earth Manual of Feng Shui*, London, 1982.

Van Over, Raymond, *I-Ching*, Chicago, 1971.

Wilhelm, Richard, *I-Ching*, London, 1951.

Willets, William, *Chinese Art*, London, 1958.

**Other books on Chinese subjects published by
Times Books International:**

Chinese Brushpainting: A Beginner's Guide, by Joseph Chan. Trains
the beginner to develop a reasoning mentality in approaching the art.
Includes step-by-step illustrations of common brush strokes and
explanations.

Chinese Geomancy, by Evelyn Lip. A layman's guide to the history and
theory of geomancy.

Chinese Numbers—Significance, Symbolism and Traditions, by
Evelyn Lip. This book reveals the meanings and usages of numbers
and the superstitions surrounding them in Chinese culture.

Choosing Auspicious Chinese Names, by Evelyn Lip. A guide for every
Chinese parent on choosing the right name for their baby, based on
ancient Chinese theories.

Feng Shui for Business, by Evelyn Lip. A guide for those who are
starting a new business, setting up shops, hotels, shopping or office
complexes or factories, to tap the good cosmic energy of the earth.

The Chinese Art of Face Reading, by Evelyn Lip. An introduction to the
Chinese art of face reading, showing how facial features influence
fortune and what they reveal of personality traits.

Understanding Jade – A Layman's Guide, by Lee Siow Mong. A guide
to identifying, caring for and selecting a piece of jade. With
descriptions of historical pieces, art, objects, beliefs, myths and
magical qualities.